Holmes McDougall: History 11-13

Studies in Evidence 1

Prehistoric Britain

Ian Dawson

General Editor:
Tony Boddington

Stonehenge today from the air

Contents

Designed by Pat Macdonald

All artwork by Rosalind Lobb, except pp. 20, 21, 32, 37, 48 by Nancy Bryce, p. 47 by Harry Trowell

ISBN 0 7157 2133-X

© Ian Dawson 1983. Printed and published by Holmes McDougall Ltd., Allander House, 137-141 Leith Walk, Edinburgh EH6 8NS.

1: Stonehenge

Country people often used Stonehenge as a meeting-place before they went hunting. This picture shows hare-coursers of the late nineteenth century using Stonehenge as a venue.

Stonehenge as it is today. What questions do you want to ask about it?

Did you recognise the photograph on the cover of this book? As soon as you saw it, you probably said to yourself, 'That's Stonehenge'. For Stonehenge is not only the most famous prehistoric building in Britain, it is one of the best known sights in the world. Many places are famed for their size or their beauty or their age, but Stonehenge is a little different. Like the pyramids of Egypt, Stonehenge has the added attraction of mystery.

This mystery has brought people to Stonehenge for centuries. The oldest picture we have of Stonehenge was drawn in the fourteenth century, but it was in the 1600s that large numbers of people began to travel to see it. Nowadays as many as three-quarters of a million people visit Stonehenge each year. This great number of tourists is a problem. There is a danger of damage to the great stones, so people are asked to be as careful as possible.

Visitors have not always been careful, as you can guess from the picture. Many of the stones have been damaged, sometimes by souvenir-hunters. People have hacked off lumps of stone to take home to show to their friends. A local blacksmith in the nineteenth century made money by hiring out hammers to these vandals. Some of the original stones have completely disappeared. Local people used them to repair roads and gateways!

If you have been to Stonehenge, you will remember what you thought and felt as you stood amongst the great stones. Perhaps you felt excited. Strangely, some people are a little disappointed. Above all, nearly everybody is puzzled. Whether you've been there or just looked at pictures, all sorts of questions will occur to you. What questions would you like to ask about Stonehenge?

Of all the questions asked about Stonehenge the most puzzling is, 'Why was it built?' There have been many different answers to this question. Here are a few of the most interesting:

The dancing giants

The picture may help you to understand this idea. Hundreds of years ago, people could not believe that ordinary men and women had built Stonehenge. Their only answer to the problem was that Stonehenge had been made by magic. They believed that the stones were the remains of giants who had been turned to stone while dancing.

The dancing giants turned to stone. This is a seventeenth-century picture.

Merlin's war memorial

Ambrosius, King of the Britons around AD 450, wanted to build a memorial to his soldiers who had died fighting the Saxons. Geoffrey of Monmouth, writing in the twelfth century, explained how Merlin solved Ambrosius's problem:

' "If you want to grace the burial-place of these men with some lasting monument," replied Merlin, "send for the Giant's Ring which is . . . in Ireland. . . . The stones are enormous and there is no-one alive strong enough to move them. If they are placed in position round this site, in the way in which they are erected over there, they will stand for ever." The king agreed with Merlin's plan, and so Merlin used his magic to move the stones and rebuild them as Stonehenge.'

A Roman temple

Several new ideas about Stonehenge were put forward in the 1600s. One of these came from Inigo Jones, a famous architect, who was asked by King James VI and I to make a full study of Stonehenge. Jones had visited many old buildings in Europe. He decided that only the Romans had enough 'knowledge and experience in all Arts and Science' to build Stonehenge. His idea of Stonehenge as a Roman temple built between AD 50 and AD 400 is shown in the picture here. Jones also believed that the Romans worshipped the God of the Sky and that bulls or oxen were sacrificed there.

This is Stonehenge as Inigo Jones imagined it had once been – a Roman temple.

A Danish king is crowned. Charleton imagined that Stonehenge had been used for this kind of ceremony.

A Danish parliament

A seventeenth-century scientist, Dr Walter Charleton, disagreed with Jones. He thought that Stonehenge was very like monuments he had seen in Denmark. He decided that the Danes had built Stonehenge between AD 800 and AD 1050 after they had invaded England. Charleton thought they had used Stonehenge as a kind of parliament and as a place for electing their kings. He pictured the new leader standing on the highest stone so that the people could see him.

A Druid temple

A man called William Stukeley, writing in the 1740s, made the connection between Stonehenge and the Druids. The picture shows the kind of scenes Stukeley imagined. He said that Stonehenge and other stone circles were built as temples where the Druids worshipped serpents and made sacrifices. The Druids were the priests of the British tribes who ruled Britain before the Romans invaded in AD 43. Modern 'Druids' still act out their ceremonies on mid-summer's day.

Another possible use for Stonehenge — a Druid temple

A prehistoric tribal centre

More recently, it has been suggested that Stonehenge was the meeting-place for tribes from a wide area. People may have gathered there to celebrate the rising of the sun at mid-summer and to pray for good harvests. Because so many people came together at mid-summer it may also have been a political meeting-place and a market-place where traders sold their goods.

The ideas on the last two pages show you that people have thought of very different reasons for the building of Stonehenge. How do you decide which of these ideas are unlikely and which could be correct? You could use the picture on the cover to help you. Do all the ideas seem sensible ones? Or can you use your common sense to rule out some of them? Look again at the pictures of Stonehenge. Are the stones really the remains of dancing giants?

If you use information from the site to help to answer your question, you are using the same method as historians and archaeologists. When they have a problem they always look for clues at the site they are investigating.

On these pages you can see some of the very straightforward clues from Stonehenge — the stones and a ground-plan of the site. Do you think that the people who thought of the six ideas on pages 4-5 used clues from the site? Did they see something at Stonehenge that made them think, 'Yes, that's why they built this place!'?

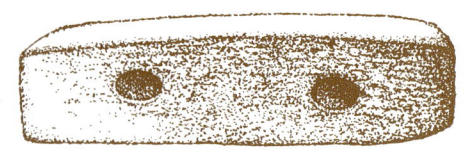

This is one of the lintel stones (the stones that lay on top of the standing stones). The underside had holes carved in it while the standing stones (see below) had a point on the top. The point fitted into the hole, which made the two stones secure.

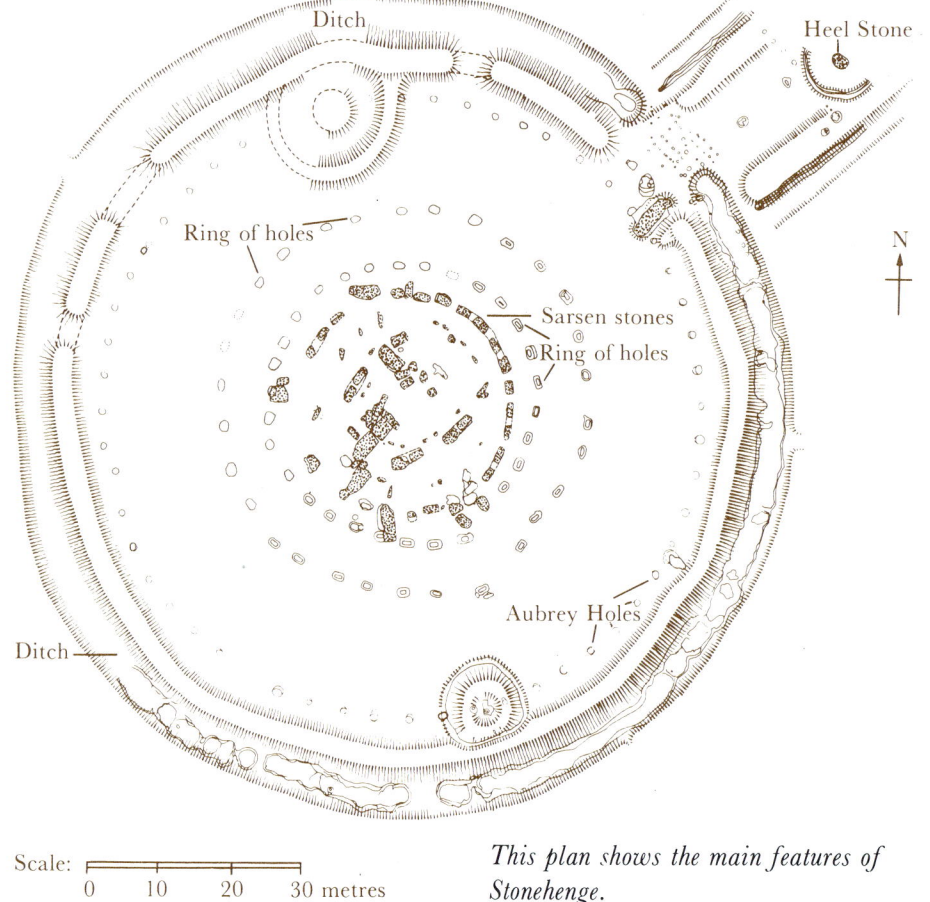

Scale:
0   10   20   30 metres

This plan shows the main features of Stonehenge.

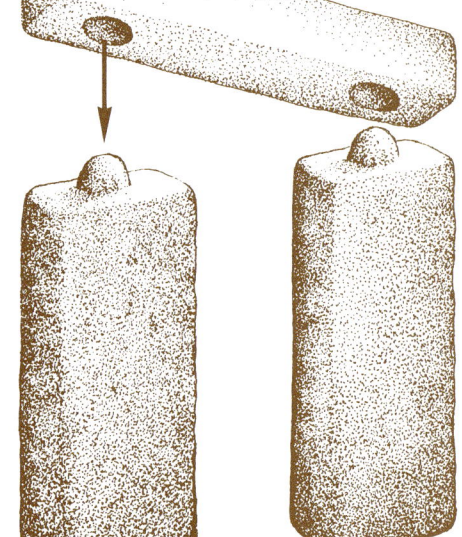

This group of stones is called a trilithon. How old do you think it is?

So far we have looked at only one question about Stonehenge, but there are lots of other questions people ask. Another very common question is, 'When was Stonehenge built?'

Finding out when something was built is usually quite easy, even when a building is very old. From the style of a building, historians can tell roughly when it was built. They can sometimes obtain more exact information from written records. For example, English government papers tell us that in 1323 King Edward II ordered the building at Pickering castle of 'a barbican before the Castle gate with a stone wall and a gate with a drawbridge . . . and beyond the gate a new chamber.'

For later buildings we often have the plans of the architect or the diaries or letters of the owner. Some builders have even been kind enough to put the date of buildings above the front door!

These are some of the different kinds of clues that tell us when buildings were put up, but we don't have these simple clues for Stonehenge. However, historians and archaeologists think that they do know when Stonehenge was built. They have looked carefully at the site and have used new scientific techniques to help to explain the clues they have found. The illustrations on the next two pages explain their ideas.

A group of sarsens (sandstone boulders) with the lintels still in place

The dating of Stonehenge

There are two main ways of deciding when Stonehenge was built. One is a scientific method called radio-carbon dating; the other method is to compare things found at Stonehenge with finds from other sites.

Radio-carbon dating is a scientific method which has been in use only since the 1950s. It can measure the age of animal and vegetable matter, that is things that were once living and growing, such as animal bones, antlers, wood and plants. When a pick made out of a deer's antler was found, radio-carbon dating showed that it was almost 5000 years old. This was very important because the pick was found at the bottom of the ditch, covered by centuries of earth and rubbish. This pick must have been used to dig the ditch, the very earliest part of Stonehenge, about 2800 BC. Perhaps a careless worker dropped it 5000 years ago, and so gave us a very important clue.

Radio-carbon dating has also shown that Stonehenge was built in five stages. We now know that stage 2 lasted only a century before it was greatly altered. Then there was a much longer period before any more changes were made. It was about another 500 years before stage 4 was built.

Using the second dating method, archaeologists have compared pottery from Stonehenge with pottery from other sites which were used at the same times. For example, pieces of pottery were found at Stonehenge mixed with chips of the bluestones that were used in the 'horseshoes' of stage 2. Archaeologists know that this type of pottery was used in other places around 2500-2000 BC. Therefore, stage 2 of Stonehenge was built during the same period.

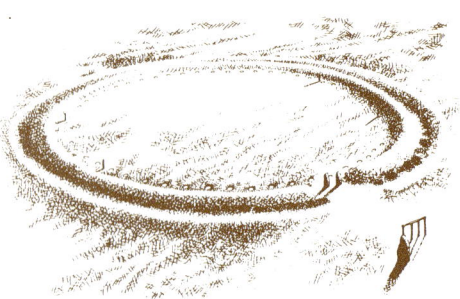

Stage 1 of the construction of Stonehenge was finished about 2800 BC. The ditch was dug and the earth was used to build the banks. A circle of holes (now known as the Aubrey Holes after the man who discovered them) was dug and the Heel Stone was put up beside a wooden gateway.

In stage 2 (around 2100 BC) the banks were made to form 'the Avenue'. Eighty stones called 'bluestones' were put up in the shape of two horseshoes. Three larger stones were added. These point towards the mid-summer sunrise.

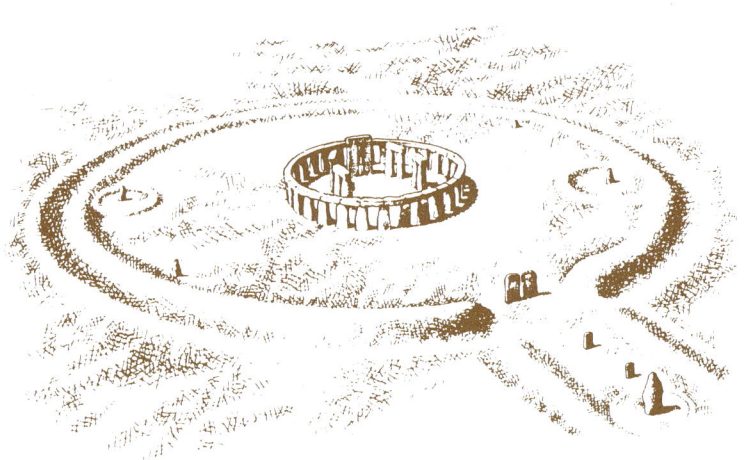

In stage 3, about 100 years later, there was a complete change. The bluestones were dug up and replaced by the circle of sarsens. Inside this circle was a horseshoe of trilithons.

Around 1550 BC, in stage 4, more than twenty of the bluestones were used again to make a circle in the very centre of Stonehenge.

Stage 5 followed almost immediately. The circle of bluestones was changed into a horseshoe and an outer circle of bluestones was added.

We have just seen how archaeologists have used clues to answer the question, 'When was Stonehenge built?' These clues can also help us with our first question, 'Why was Stonehenge built?' We know that Stonehenge was built between 2800 BC and 1500 BC. This means that some of the ideas on pages 4 and 5 must be wrong. Look again at those six explanations. Which of them can you now rule out because of the dates when Stonehenge was built?

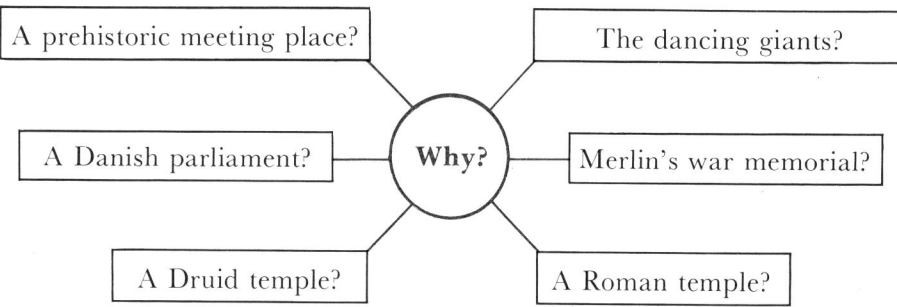

Stonehenge, built 2800-1500 BC

A prehistoric meeting place?

The dancing giants?

A Danish parliament?

Why?

Merlin's war memorial?

A Druid temple?

A Roman temple?

Direction of mid-summer sunrise (towards Heel Stone)

Direction of mid-winter sunset

Scale:

0   10   20   30 metres

N

Stonehenge points out the place where the sun rises at mid-summer. But does it do more?

How many of the six ideas are left? Even if there is only one left, is there enough information to prove that it's the right answer?

If there aren't enough clues to help to answer a question, people will keep thinking of new ideas. Recently a new and complicated answer has been given to the question 'Why was Stonehenge built?'

For a long time people have connected Stonehenge with the worship of the sun. This is why there are 'Druid' ceremonies at Stonehenge every mid-summer, when 'Druids' go there to celebrate the rising of the sun on the longest day of the year. If you stand in the centre of the circle and face towards the Heel Stone (look at the plan of Stonehenge on page 6) you are looking towards the point where the sun rises on mid-summer's day.

The position of the sunrise has been known for a long time. Recently some people have said that Stonehenge was built to do more than mark the rise of the mid-summer sun. They believe that it was an observatory for viewing both the sun and the moon and that it recorded their movements in the sky. It has also been said that the Aubrey Holes (shown in the plan on page 6) could be used to predict eclipses.

Modern 'Druids' celebrating mid-summer at Stonehenge

The scientists who worked out these ideas used a computer to help them. The computer worked out the results using the clues from Stonehenge — the stones themselves, their size and the distances between them.

Even if Stonehenge does show the movements of the sun and moon, is this really why it was built? You might think that this is the probable reason but you cannot be certain. There are no definite clues which tell us why Stonehenge was built. Nobody will ever solve finally the mystery of Stonehenge.

Alan Sorrell's idea of Stonehenge as it was 3500 years ago. How did he decide that it looked like this?

The questions we have asked about Stonehenge are the same questions that archaeologists and historians ask about any event or period in the past. These are the three main questions:

When did this happen?
The historians' first task is to decide when something happened. They also try to work out the order of events.

How did people live then?
Historians try to show us how people lived at different times in the past, and in what ways their lives were the same as ours or different from ours. To do this, historians might look at the homes and clothes of people from a different time, together with their food, the work they did, and their religion.

Archaeologists and historians use this information to build up a picture of the lives of people in the past. They usually do this in words, but an artist called Alan Sorrell has based his drawings (like the one on page 11) on historical information. These drawings help to show you how people lived long ago. If you thought that Stone-Age people lived just like us in the twentieth century, you probably wouldn't think that the cartoon below was very funny.

'Course, it'll be better when we've got the curtains up.'

Why did people do certain things?
This is the hardest of the three questions. To answer it, we need to find out about other people's ideas and the way they thought. This is not easy, because prehistoric people left no simple clues, such as letters or books, to explain their thoughts and ideas. Without this kind of clue it is very difficult to answer questions like 'Why was Stonehenge built?'

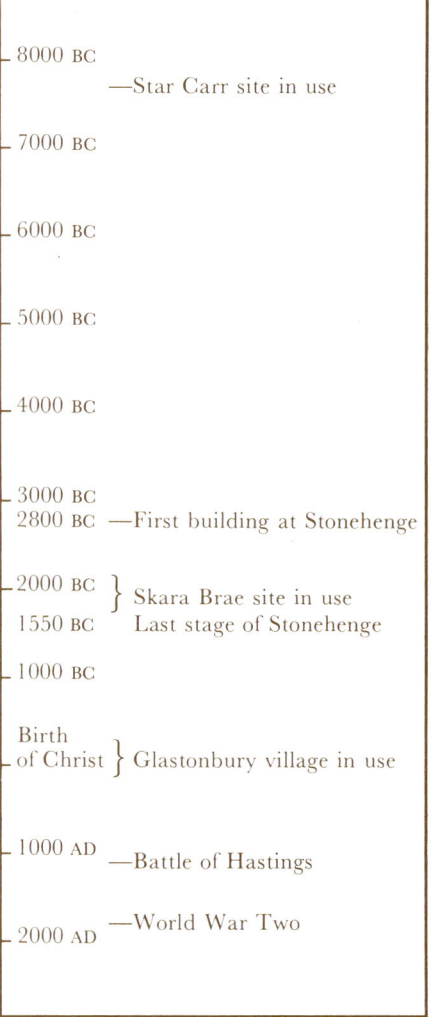

8000 BC
—Star Carr site in use

7000 BC

6000 BC

5000 BC

4000 BC

3000 BC
2800 BC —First building at Stonehenge

2000 BC } Skara Brae site in use
1550 BC   Last stage of Stonehenge

1000 BC

Birth
of Christ } Glastonbury village in use

1000 AD —Battle of Hastings

2000 AD —World War Two

Here you can see when the sites were lived in or used.

12

2: Star Carr

You probably decided that Stonehenge was used for special meetings. On these occasions groups of people gathered from far and near, often travelling for days to get there. They may have come together for a religious ceremony, to worship the sun. They may have prayed to their gods for good crops in the coming year. They might have come to Stonehenge to check the movements of the sun and the moon by the great stones. Perhaps it was a mixture of all these.

Although many people visited Stonehenge, nobody lived there. We know this because there are no clues about everyday life. If people had lived there we would expect to see signs of their houses. There would be many animal bones from their food, and there would be many pieces of pottery. There are none of these. Stonehenge tells us little about everyday life in prehistoric Britain.

To find out how people lived in prehistoric Britain we must look in other places. In the rest of this book we shall look at the information from three other sites: Star Carr in Yorkshire, Skara Brae in Orkney, and Glastonbury in Somerset. These sites will tell us a good deal about the lives of people who lived in Britain thousands of years ago.

Sometimes great discoveries about the past have been accidental. A farmer's tractor has dug up a forgotten treasure, children exploring caves have come across ancient cave paintings. More often, archaeologists have good reasons for looking in a certain place. Certain clues at Star Carr made archaeologists think that this would be a good place to excavate.

This map shows the four sites we are investigating in this book. There are many other prehistoric sites open to visitors. If you live near one of them, try to visit it to examine for yourself the different kinds of evidence from prehistoric Britain. Visiting a site is much more exciting than reading about it!

13

In the late 1940s, a group of British archaeologists were interested in hunting life about 10 000 years ago. Archaeologists had found plenty of information about hunters in Europe but they had found nothing in Britain. British archaeologists wanted to find a hunters' camp in their own country.

The archaeologists knew the kind of place to explore. Most objects made around 8000 BC would have rotted away many years ago. However, wooden and other objects can survive if they are buried in wet, marshy ground. So the archaeologists looked close to marshland for signs of hunting, such as flint weapons and pieces of bone. When a large number of flints were found at Star Carr in Yorkshire, excavations began which lasted for three years.

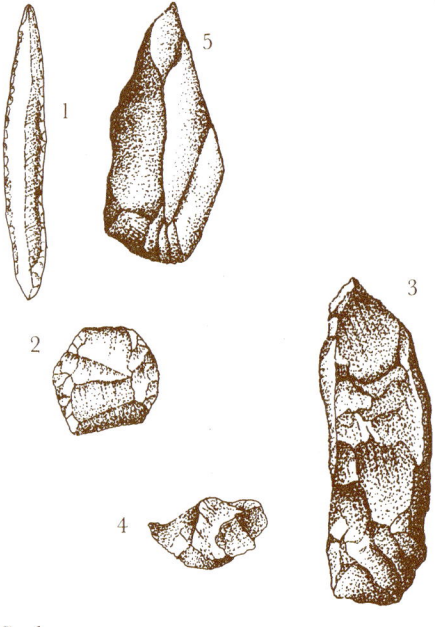

A section of the flooring at Star Carr. Stones and lumps of clay were added to the wooden base.

This dig proved to be very important. Star Carr was the first hunters' settlement found in Britain. The next few pages will show you how much you can learn from Star Carr about the lives of the people in Britain 8000 years BC. What would you expect to find out about these people?

In the last section we looked at the kinds of questions historians and archaeologists ask. First, they would want to know when people lived at Star Carr. Then historians would ask about their way of life, their houses, clothes and food, how they hunted and the number of people in the group. You have probably thought of a lot more questions. We will now see which of these questions archaeologists were able to answer from the clues at Star Carr.

Scale: |⎯⎯⎯⎯⎯⎯⎯⎯⎯⎯⎯⎯⎯⎯|
0   5 cm

Flint tools found at Star Carr. These sketches are smaller than the actual flints. They are: an awl (1), a scraper (2), an axe or adze blade (3) and sharpening flake (4), and a burin (5), which was used by engravers.

When did people live at Star Carr?

The mud layer which preserved many objects of wood, bone and antler gave the answer. Radio-carbon dating of these articles showed that the site was used around 7600 BC.

How large was this camp?

The chart below gives you the clues to answer this question. Over 17 000 flints were found in the camp. Here you can see how these flints were spread around the site. How would you use this information to decide how large the camp was? After you have answered this question, try to work out how many people might have lived in such a space.

This is a plan of the Star Carr camp-site. Archaeologists use plans like this to record exactly where they find things – this one shows how many flints were found in each part of the site. (The thick black line shows the extent of the excavation.) Can you work out anything else from this plan?

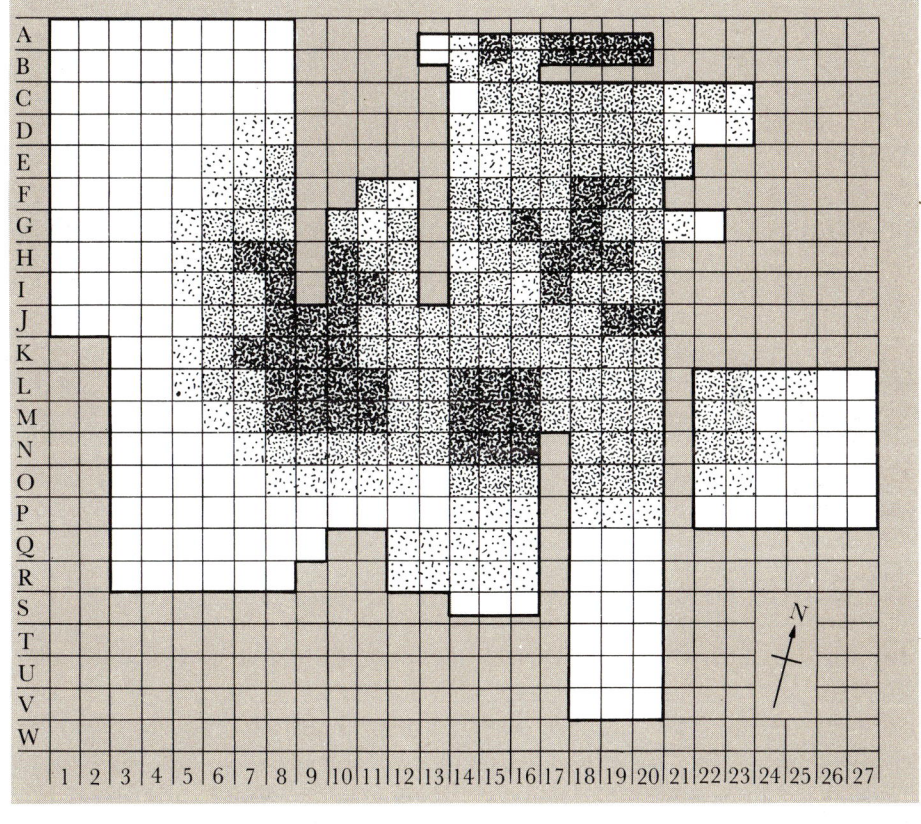

Scale: ☐ 1 square metre

Key to number of worked flints:

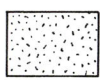 0-17 per square metre   18+ per square metre 36+ per square metre 90+ per square metre

What kind of shelter did these people have?

Another way to see how many people lived at Star Carr would be to find out how many houses or shelters there were. However, there was no information about their shelters. Why was this?

This camp was sited next to a lake. The ground must have been very soggy because the people who lived there put down a layer of brushwood as a kind of platform. This reached to the lakeside where it acted as a landing stage. All the objects that have been found had fallen into or below this platform, usually by accident. Anything above it has been lost by decay. Therefore, any skin tents or reed huts disappeared long ago.

The timber flooring of the site. It is almost 10 000 years old.

Red deer

Roe deer

Why didn't these people build stronger houses?

The answer is that they didn't live at Star Carr all the year round. They camped there only in winter and early spring before moving on to hunt somewhere else. The size of deer antlers found at the site told the archaeologists when the camp was used. The antlers were quite small, which means that the Star Carr people collected them in the winter and early spring. However, each year for a number of years, they came back to Star Carr. We know this because so many animal bones were found. The tribe could not have eaten so much meat in one season.

What did these people eat?

The main clues used by the archaeologists to answer this question were the animal bones found at the site. These have survived well in the marshy conditions. You would probably expect these lakeside dwellers to have eaten plenty of fish but no fish bones have remained. This is because fish bones decay very quickly. The bones of a small number of sea birds were found but in nothing like the quantities of the land animals.

From the number of bones, archaeologists worked out how many animals of each kind there were. The chart shows how much meat these animals provided. The red deer provided most of the meat eaten around the camp fire, followed by the much larger and heavier oxen. As you can see, many roe deer were killed, but because they are much smaller they provided far less meat. Pigs were a fairly unimportant part of the menu. Many bones were found broken open so that the marrow could be removed and eaten.

Some of the animals that were hunted at Star Carr: red deer, elk, roe deer and pig

These graphs show which animals were most important to the hunters of Star Carr.

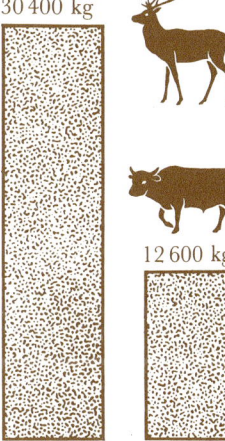   

	30 400 kg	12 600 kg	4400 kg	1518 kg	890 kg
	Red deer	Oxen	Elk	Roe deer	Pig
	160 animals	18 animals	22 animals	66 animals	10 animals

There was no sign that these people deliberately grew crops, but this isn't surprising if they used the site for only part of the year. However, the remains of wild plants and woodland fruits show that they did gather and eat natural crops. How important these were in their diet we cannot tell, as much of the plant evidence has rotted away.

From the large numbers of bones, together with other clues, archaeologists believe that a great deal of the group's time was spent on hunting and gathering food.

What kinds of tools and implements did they use?

The archaeologists found large numbers of tools and weapons preserved at Star Carr. Just as valuable was the great quantity of waste material from flints, antlers and bones. This gave a lot of information about the way the people of Star Carr made their tools and weapons.

The basic craft was making implements from flint. The flint items were used to fell trees and cut brushwood, scrape skins and make ornaments. Most importantly, flints were good for arrow tips and barbs and were used to make other tools and weapons from antlers and bones. Many of the flint items would have had wooden handles but these have decayed. However, the type of glue used to attach the handle to the flint has been found on one flint.

The second main raw material used was antler. Splinters were cut from red deer antlers with sharp flints. The people used these splinters to make barbed spearheads for hunting. Elk antlers were used as mattocks (a kind of pickaxe) for digging and grubbing up roots. You can see the holes for attaching handles in the pictures.

Bone was used much less, mainly in tools for working and scraping skins. It was also useful for making the kinds of pins and bodkins shown in the pictures.

Later peoples developed specialist skills — perhaps one or two people would make all the flint tools for the tribe. The group at Star Carr was probably too small for such specialism and everyone would have been involved in tool-making as well as in hunting.

This is how a Star Carr person would have made a hand axe. The flint was struck repeatedly on each edge to make a sharp cutting surface.

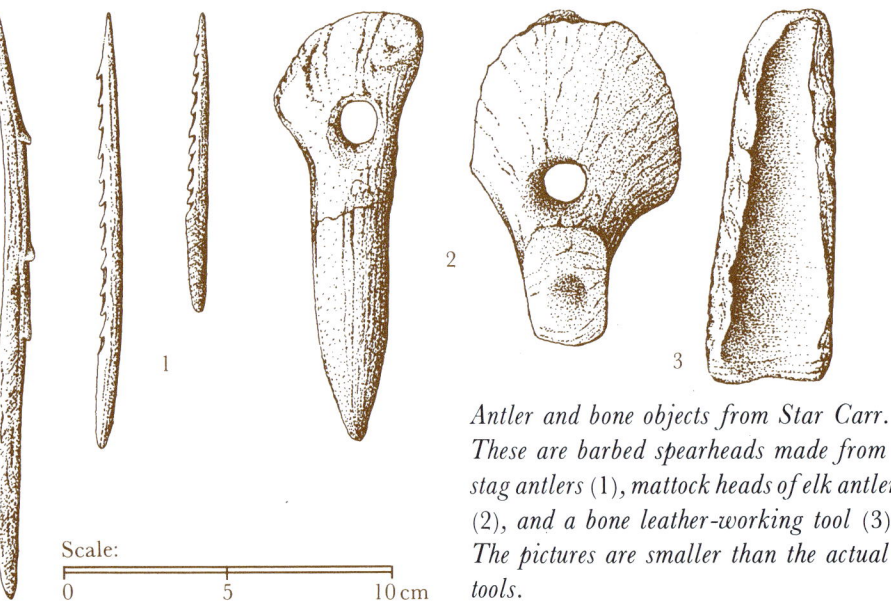

Scale:
0   5   10 cm

Antler and bone objects from Star Carr. These are barbed spearheads made from stag antlers (1), mattock heads of elk antler (2), and a bone leather-working tool (3). The pictures are smaller than the actual tools.

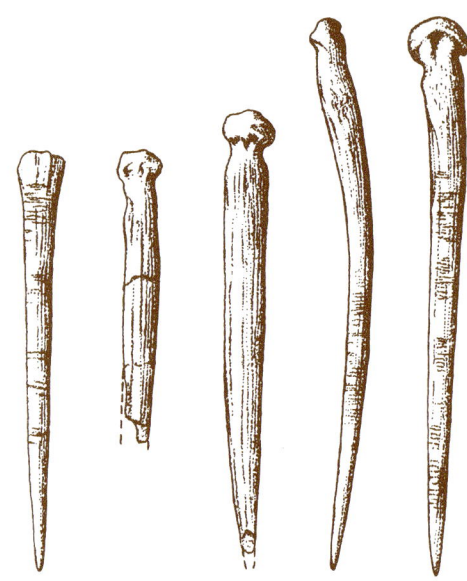

Bodkins (large needles) made from the bones of elk. They are shown 1·5 times the actual size.

18

What else was found?

We have already seen that a brushwood platform covered the site when it was in use. Two birch trees were found at the lakeside edge of this platform. These may have been a simple landing stage. It was clear that someone had felled these trees deliberately, which proves the value of the flint tools.

The only important wooden object found was the middle section of a paddle, which suggests that these people did use boats as transport. The local trees weren't suitable for making dug-out canoes so boats were probably made of skin. This would explain why no boats were found, because skin boats would have decayed quickly. One further unanswered question is whether the people at Star Carr used boats just for fishing or whether they travelled long distances in them.

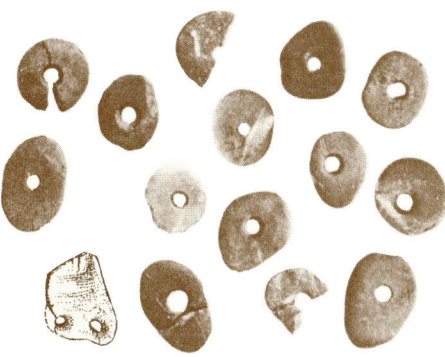

The two birch trees that were used as a landing stage

The only wooden tool found – a paddle

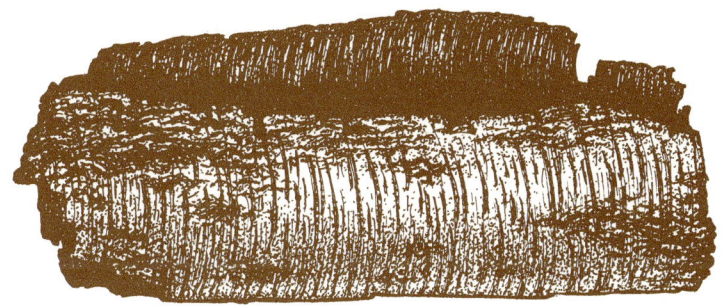

The rolled-up birch bark. These rolls puzzled the archaeologists for a long time.

Also puzzling were rolls of bark that had been stripped from birch trees. The largest was a strip 76 centimetres long and 20 centimetres across. The rolls seem to have been the method of storing the bark before it was used. But what was it used for? The clue was found on a flint. This bark, it seems, was made into the glue or resin which fixed the flint tools and weapons to their wooden handles.

Archaeologists also found a few varied articles which must have been used as 'jewellery'. These were small stone discs, about the size of a fingernail, which possibly were threaded together to act as a necklace. Pieces of amber and even teeth may have been used in necklaces or as lucky charms.

Stone discs and an amber bead. The Star Carr people used these as jewellery.

Perhaps the most interesting find of all was a group of at least twenty stag headpieces. The Star Carr people had made these into masks. The antlers were taken from mature but young stags. These gave a good set of antlers that were not too heavy. A lot of hollowing-out had been done, cutting down the weight to perhaps one-third or one-quarter of the original weight. Any rough surfaces were smoothed out and holes were made to take thongs.

What were these headpieces used for? Two answers have been put forward. One idea is that hunters used them to fool the deer and get close enough to make a kill. Until this century Eskimos used antler masks for hunting.

A second idea is that they were used at magical ceremonies. Perhaps the men acted out a hunt or performed a dance before they began the hunt. They would hope this would bring them good luck. Antler masks have been used in this way in modern times by the Tungu people of Siberia.

On these pages an artist shows how the antler headpiece (above) *may have been used. Do you agree with one or both ideas?*

Which questions could not be answered?

We have seen that the archaeologists found out a great deal about the people who lived at Star Carr ten thousand years ago. They used the clues from the site to tell them how many people lived at the site, what they ate, and what kinds of tools and weapons they used.

A number of questions could not be answered definitely. We don't know exactly what kind of shelters they had, nor what kinds of clothes they wore. However, clues can help us get close to an answer.

Two clues suggest the kind of clothing worn by the Star Carr hunters. First, we know that the July temperature was only about 12°C at that time, much cooler than nowadays. The winters must have been much colder, so the people did need clothes. Second, the archaeologists found many flints that were useful for cleaning and shaping skins. Therefore, the people were able to make clothes. Even if no clothing has survived, we can be fairly certain that the Star Carr people wore clothes made from animal skins.

Some other questions cannot be answered at all. There are no clues to help with such questions as, 'What kind of language did they use?', 'Did they believe in any gods?', 'Did the women do the same kind of work as the men?'

How did archaeologists and historians use the information they found?

They aimed to show others how the people at Star Carr lived their lives. One way to do this was to write a description of their finds, giving all the information. Readers could then use their imaginations to picture the scene.

Building up a picture for yourself, however, is very difficult. A more helpful method is for archaeologists to make a drawing of the site based on the clues found there. Here is such a drawing of Star Carr, by Alan Sorrell.

Sorrell used the clues we have looked at on the last few pages. How accurate do you think his drawing is? To decide, you may find it helpful to think about these questions:

Where has Sorrell used the clues exactly as they were found?

Where has he added a little to make sense of the clues?

Where has he invented things because there are no clues?

The last question shows one of the great problems for archaeologists and historians. There are often gaps in the information from a site. Can they be filled from other sources? Archaeologists can look at other sites from the same period, as two groups of people might well have lived in the same way. Archaeologists can also look for people today who live in a similar way to people from the past. We have seen that the Star Carr people have been compared to Eskimos and the Tungu of Siberia.

A modern Eskimo. Archaeologists and historians learned of a probable use of the Star Carr antler masks from the Eskimos.

Alan Sorrell's re-creation of the Star Carr site. Has he used the information well?

3: Skara Brae

We have looked closely at the way archaeologists used the clues from Star Carr to build up a picture of life at the site. When an archaeologist is describing the lives of people long ago he constantly refers to these clues. This is because he is using them as *evidence*.

Where else have you come across the word 'evidence'? Probably in books, films or television programmes about the police and court cases. Lawyers do not just tell a story in court and expect the jury to believe them. They bring in witnesses and documents as evidence to support what they say. Without these clues as evidence nobody would know whether to believe them or not.

Historians and archaeologists work in a similar way. How do you know Sorrell's drawing of life at Star Carr is a good one? You must check the clues and ask, 'Has he used the clues from the site as evidence for his drawing?'

Historians describing life in the past must include their evidence so that the readers know that they aren't just inventing a story. If there are no clues to act as evidence, the historians say so. They explain to their readers that they cannot be sure about certain things.

Other writers need not be so exact. A story written for entertainment does not include careful notes about clues and evidence. A novelist may base a story on historical clues but can use his or her imagination to fill any gaps. In this section we will look at the way a fiction writer has used evidence from the past to reconstruct a story about the prehistoric village of Skara Brae in Orkney.

Nobody knew anything about this village until a great storm swept over Orkney in about 1850. The storm blew away part of the sand dunes that had covered the site. Several houses could then be seen below the sand. Once this lucky find was made, the rest of the site was slowly uncovered by local people. The major excavation was completed in the 1920s.

The people and village of Skara Brae interested a writer called Kathleen Fidler. She wrote a book about them called *The Boy with the Bronze Axe*. On the next page is an outline of her story.

In the rest of this section we will compare the clues found by the archaeologists with the story written by Kathleen Fidler. You will be able to see where she has used the clues and where she has had to use her imagination.

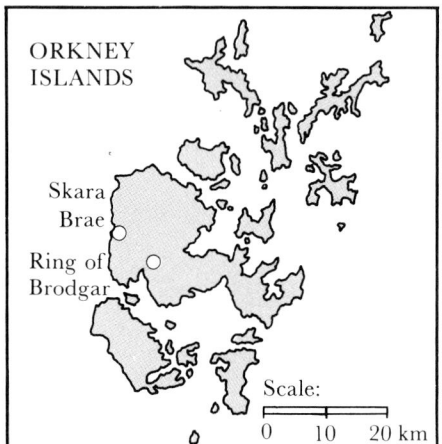

Skara Brae lies on the main island of Orkney. The village lies 8 kilometres from the Ring of Brodgar.

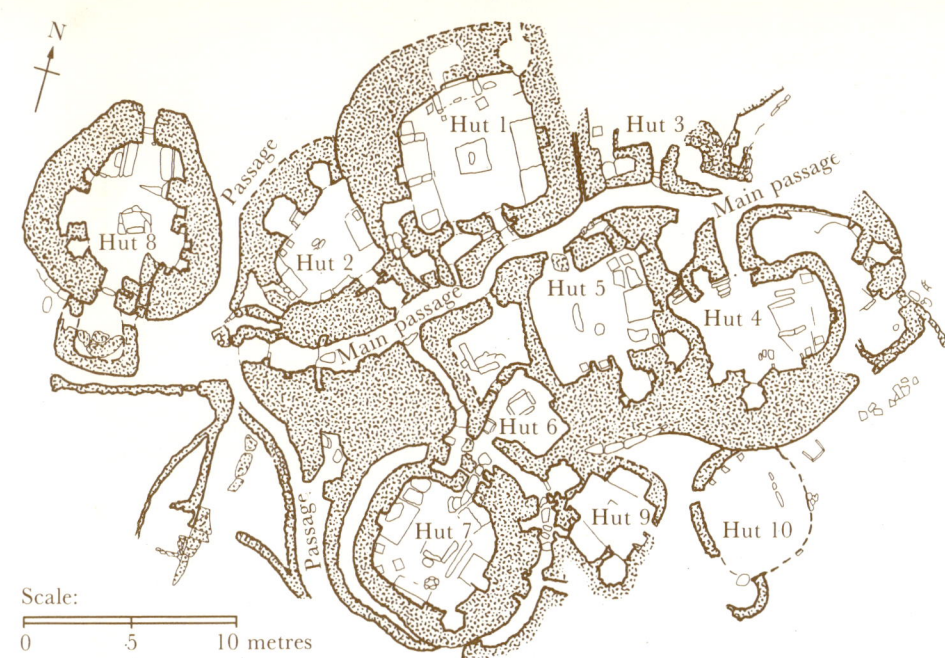

A plan of the Skara Brae site showing the huts and passages

The Boy with the Bronze Axe

Two of the main characters are Kali and Brockan, the children of Birno, the leader of the Skara Brae people. Early in the story the two children are saved from drowning by a stranger, a boy called Tenko, who owns a bronze axe. The people of Skara Brae have not learned to use metals so they find the bronze axe very strange. Tenko is accepted by the Skara Brae people after he kills an eagle which had been stealing the tribe's lambs. Tenko then takes part in the annual ceremony of the Festival of the Sun. The story ends when the village is destroyed in a great storm. Many villagers die. Tenko and Birno's family survive but can no longer live at Skara Brae.

Skara Brae as it looks today

The village and houses of Skara Brae

Radio-carbon dating tells us that people lived in the village of Skara Brae about 2000 BC. It contains between six and eight households, connected by a covered alley. The village was protected from all but the fiercest winds by a huge covering of rubbish. This was made up of peat-ash, dung, bones and shells, pieces of pottery, and other waste.

Here are some extracts from *The Boy with the Bronze Axe* which describe the village and its houses:

(A) 'Kali sat up in her stone bed filled with heather. . . . Her mother still slept in the stone bed-place on the other side of the hearth.'

(B) 'The two children tip-toed to the narrow entrance [of their hut] and Kali stooped under the stone doorway to the passage beyond. The entrance to the passage was closed by a slab of stone held in place by a stone bar fixed into holes on each side of the wall. . . . Quietly they crept along the passage which . . . led upwards and outwards to the daylight. They stood on the sand-dune that lay about their house, almost level with the beehive-like roofs of the stone village.'

(C) 'Tenko looked about him. Bone rafters made the roof, and turfs had been laid upon them to thatch them, but a large hole had been left above the hearth for a chimney. At one side of the hut was a stone dresser built of flat slabs resting on pillars of stone.'

Two views of hut 1 after it had been excavated. Was this the home of Kali and Brockan?

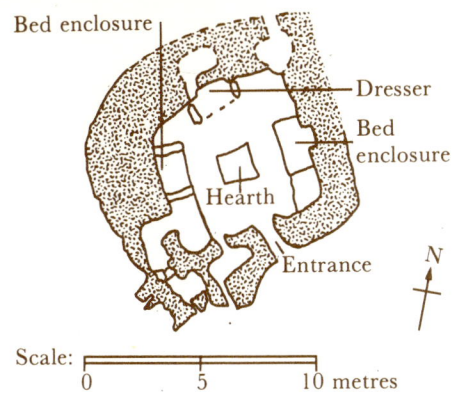

Bed enclosure

Dresser

Bed enclosure

Hearth

Entrance

N

Scale:

0 5 10 metres

A plan of hut 1. This may help you to link the photographs and the clues.

The village and houses of Skara Brae

These extracts come from the archaeologists' report. They explain what the archaeologists found at Skara Brae. These extracts and the photographs will help you to decide how well Kathleen Fidler has used the clues to help her readers to imagine the site, and especially hut 1.

(1) 'An alternative method of roofing has been suggested by Mr Watt who found the jaw bones of a large whale lying across the hearth of hut 1 as if they had fallen in from above.'

(2) 'Access to the huts was obtained through a low, narrow tunnel-like passage. . . . The passage could be closed by a door, presumably a slab of stone that might be held in place . . . by a bar fitting into sockets in the passage wall.'

(3) 'Approximately in the centre of every hut is a rectangular enclosure about 1½ metres square, formed of four narrow slabs like kerb-stones, set on edge or laid horizontally. . . . Immediately behind the kerbed area stood a sort of hearth stone, some 45 centimetres high.'

(4) 'Built out from the wall on either side of the hearth is a pair of enclosures, each formed by two slabs on edge projecting from the side wall at right angles and a third slab joining [them]. The slabs rise from 53 cm to 86 cm above the floor. . . . The right hand enclosure is always the larger (2 metres by one metre and 7 cm in hut 1). . . . No left hand [enclosure] exceeds one metre and 67 cm in length.'

(5) 'Against the rear wall of every hut stood a curious system of one, or probably always, two shelves, supported on three stone piers. [In hut 1] the whole structure is built out from the wall.'

The passage which linked the huts of Skara Brae

27

The food, clothing and tools of the Skara Brae people

Extracts from *The Boy with the Bronze Axe*

(D) 'Kali emptied the limpets and shellfish on to a stone slab and began to scrape the limpets out of their shells into a shallow earthenware bowl. She used a tiny flint scraper as a knife. Stempsi [her mother] took the crabs and eel and wrapped them up in a covering of wet clay which she thrust into the glowing heart of the fire, prodding it into place with the long leg-bone of an ox which she used like a poker. There the shellfish would bake while they ate the raw limpets.'

(E) 'Stempsi handed the mutton bones to everyone. Earlier she had thrust the meat among the hot stones in the fire, and though the outside was scorched, the inside meat was almost raw. That did not worry anyone. The family was used to eating its meat either raw or partly burned. They all gnawed at the bones with relish, their strong white teeth tearing the meat away.'

(F) 'Birno lifted a stone axe from the keeping-place hollowed out of the wall beyond his bed. His stone axe was wedged into a piece of deer antler used as a haft. Lines were chiselled on the stone in a pleasing pattern of squares and diagonals over the centre of the axe-head.'

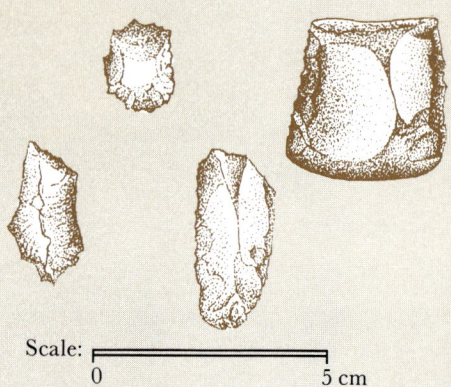

Scale: 0 — 5 cm

Small flint scrapers of this kind were found all over the site.

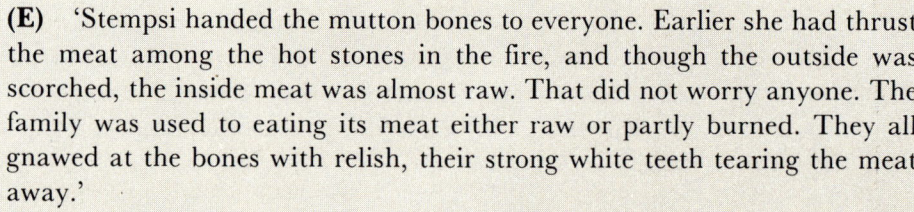

A stone tool or weapon, perhaps an axe-head or a club. The scratches in the centre may be decorations.

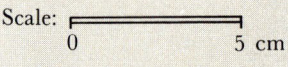

Scale: 0 — 5 cm

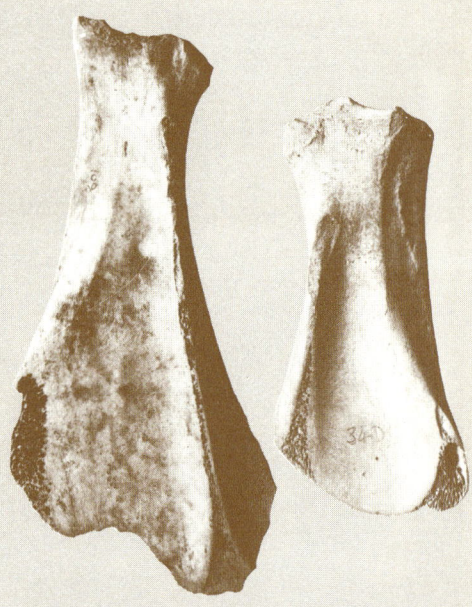

The Skara Brae people made animal bones such as these into tools. These ox bones may have been used as shovels.

28

These ox bones may have been used as adzes or axes.

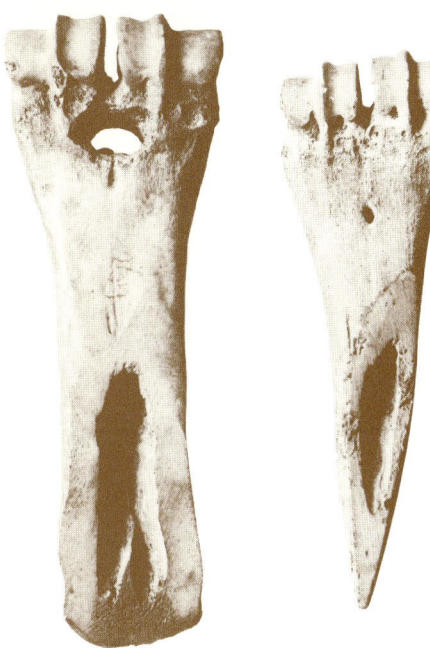

The food, clothing and tools of the Skara Brae people

Extracts from the archaeologists' report

(6) 'The basis of life at Skara Brae must have been the breeding of sheep and cattle. The bones of these animals are found in immense numbers in the midden.... Owing to the difficulty of keeping stock through the winter, male calves were slaughtered.'

(7) 'After beef and mutton, shellfish, especially limpets, figured prominently on the prehistoric menu.'

(8) 'Whalebone turned up in considerable quantities, but the amount found hardly presupposes an organised whaling industry. One or two stranded whales would provide all the material actually unearthed.'

(9) 'The bones of sheep and cattle, local . . . rocks and flint . . . provided the villagers with the materials for tools which were certainly home-made.'

(10) 'Flakes and small cores of flint . . . are plentiful all about the site, but almost the only [type of] implement made of these materials was a small round scraper. . . . [The scraper, *top-right on page 28*,] is trimmed to give scraper-edges along the sides, but the convex end is polished on both faces to produce a cutting edge.'

(11) 'Fifteen [axeheads] have been recovered from Skara Brae. . . . One . . . was of yellow flint and superbly polished.'

(12) '[Axeheads were] affixed by some means to the end of a wooden shaft. . . . One specimen . . . exhibits shallow grooves pecked out on both faces.'

(13) 'One of the actual hafts was discovered. . . . It is made from a section of antler, 7½ cm long, sawn off at both ends. The spongy interior has been removed from the lower and wider end . . . to make a socket for the [head]. . . . A transverse hole . . . pierces the antler to take the shaft.'

Scale: 0   5 cm

The haft of an adze made from antler. The shaft (handle) was fixed through the hole. The head was fixed into the wider end.

A simple but effective-looking stone implement (right)

Scale: 0   5 cm
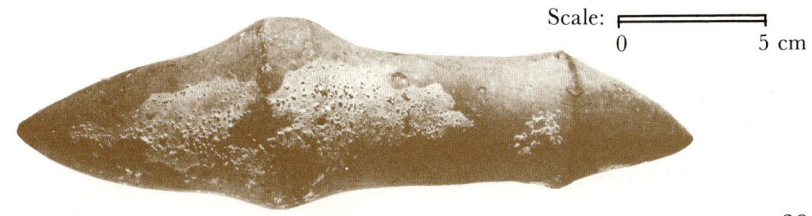

Extracts from *The Boy with the Bronze Axe*

(G) 'Some women were sitting on the sand-dunes just outside the huts. With flint scrapers they were busy scraping clean the inside of sheepskins and cow-hides. Others, with bone-needles, were piercing holes and fastening skins together by threads made from animal tendons. These would be tunics and cloaks for their families.'

(H) 'The women prepared new tunics of the softest sheepskin. With flint scrapers they scraped away the wool and washed the skins in the stream. . . . They kneaded and pounded them on the stones till the skins were soft and supple. Then they shaped them into tunics, sewing up the sides with sinews from the sheep. Kali joined the women. . . . She had begged two soft lambskins. . . . Kali sewed them into a tunic. . . . She bored holes in sheep's teeth she had collected and sewed them round the neck of the garment in a pattern. She tacked a deep pocket on the inside of the tunic and fastened it with whalebone pins.'

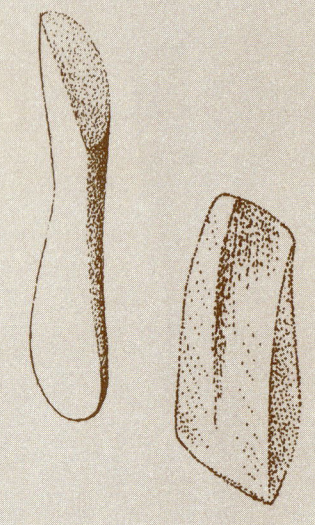

Smoothing and cutting tools made from bone

The people of Skara Brae used bone in different ways – for practical items like needles and scrapers and for decoration, in necklaces and pendants.

(I) 'He pulled out a necklace. It was made of the teeth of many animals, beautifully polished and shining white. They were graded from the very small teeth of rabbits and lambs to the larger teeth of sheep and cows. There were nearly a hundred of these ivory beads and from the centre hung two of the great teeth of the killer-whale.'

30

Extracts from the archaeologists' report

(14) 'Many of the bone tools seem well adapted to the preparation of garments from [skins and hides].'

(15) 'By far the commonest implement at Skara Brae is a pin or awl made by splitting a marrow bone . . . down the shaft. . . . The rough edges of the splinter so formed were then smoothed down and the lower end trimmed to a neat point by rubbing on a flagstone slab.'

(16) 'The villagers of Skara Brae . . . used to make serviceable, if not durable, knives from beach pebbles. If a suitably shaped pebble of flagstone be dashed on the ground at the right angle, it splits . . . yielding a flake with quite a sharp edge.'

Bone needles. They were used for making clothes from skin and hides.

Simple bone tools used for making holes in animal skins

(17) 'The villagers wore necklaces or girdles of beads and pendants. The beads were made of bone, bovine teeth, ivory, or, very rarely, of stone.'

(18) 'The leg-bones of sheep or birds provided a convenient material for beads since the marrow-cavity offers a ready-made string-hole. . . . To make the beads all that had to be done was to cut the bone up into convenient lengths.'

(19) 'The commonest pendant at Skara Brae is of the tusk type. . . . Some are carved out of larger pieces of ivory, but in others the actual teeth of killer-whales are utilised.'

An ivory pin. It is over 12 cm long – one of the largest found on the site.

31

Customs and ceremonies

Extracts from *The Boy with the Bronze Axe*

Carved stone balls, about the size of cricket balls, found at Skara Brae

(J) 'In preparation for the longest day of the year the tribe of Skara had many things to do. The previous day they cast off their old tunics and rushed into the sea. They rubbed their bodies with white sand till the skin was reddened. This was the ceremony of cleansing.

Next came the ceremony of painting. The women had prepared pigments in little basins made from the vertebrae [bones from the spine] of the whale. There was a yellow paint made from a clay ochre, a red paint made by crushing pieces of rusty-looking stone, and blue paint from a flax plant.

. . . Birno opened his tunic. Upon his chest was daubed a round red circle. "It is the mark of the Sun God. All our people carry it." '

(K) 'Birno came to the meeting place carrying six beautifully carved stone balls. These were the symbols of the Sun belonging to the tribe of Skara. . . . Two of them had been carved by Birno himself. Birno looked with pride at the last stone ball he had carved. The carving on it was so deep that the pattern stood out in spikes like a hedgehog. It had taken Birno a whole year to carve. . . . The spikes represented the rays of the sun.'

(L) 'There were two ways across the moat. . . . At the north-west crossing Birno halted and lined up his people. Only the men would cross into the sacred ring. . . . Birno . . . gave the word, "Lift up your symbols of the Sun." The six leaders held the carved stone balls high in their hands. . . . The company advanced across the earthen bridge with the signs of the Sun held aloft. . . . Three times the tribes of Orkney marched round the Ring of Brodgar and each time the men passed the highest stone of all, they lifted the signs of the Sun which they carried and shouted loudly.'

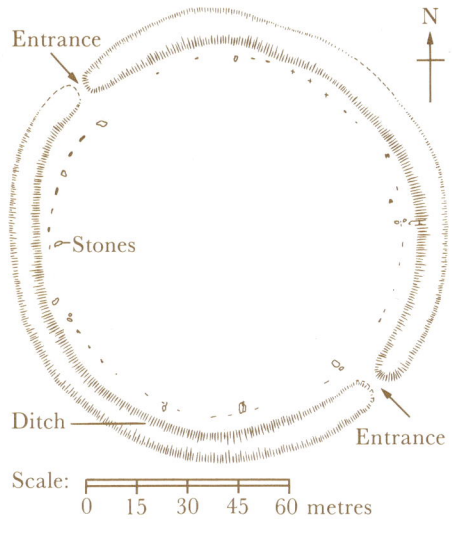

Entrance

N

Stones

Ditch

Entrance

Scale:

0   15   30   45   60 metres

Plan of the Ring of Brodgar showing the stones, ditch and entrances

The Ring of Brodgar

Customs and ceremonies

Information from the archaeologists' report

(20) The villagers used simple vessels of stone and bone made in varying sizes. Red colouring matter was frequently found in the smaller stone vessels. The small whalebone vessels also contained colouring matter.

(21) Several stone balls were found at Skara Brae. (They are shown in the pictures.) One was found in hut 2. It had been polished and a simple chequer pattern had been scratched on it. Another, found in hut 4, had been cut so that six low round shapes stood out from its surface.

The best of these stone balls was found in hut 3. Again it had been cut away to leave a series of spikes all over the surface. The grooves had been polished, probably with sand.

(22) The Ring of Brodgar had, at most, sixty standing stones. The ditch was about 9 metres wide and 2 metres deep.

On the last eight pages you have been comparing a novelist's reconstruction of life at Skara Brae with the archaeological clues. Sometimes there are plenty of clues, so the reconstruction can be very accurate. Sometimes there are only just enough clues. Then the writer has to add a little to make sense of them. At other times there are hardly any clues. Then the fiction writer can use his or her imagination to fill the gaps. But remember, historians cannot invent things to fill gaps in their writing.

Why do these gaps exist? We are dealing with a village that was lived in about 4000 years ago. In these 4000 years many remains will have rotted away. Some things we would like to know about just don't leave clues behind them. However, the way Skara Brae was buried and the wide use of stone in its building has preserved a great deal.

We will now look at one final part of the Skara Brae site. See what you can work out from the clues.

If you look back at the plan of Skara Brae on page 25 you will see that one hut, number 8, stands away from the rest. It was not covered by waste like the others. It is different in a number of ways from the other huts. The question is, what was hut 8 used for?

Let's look at the clues in hut 8.

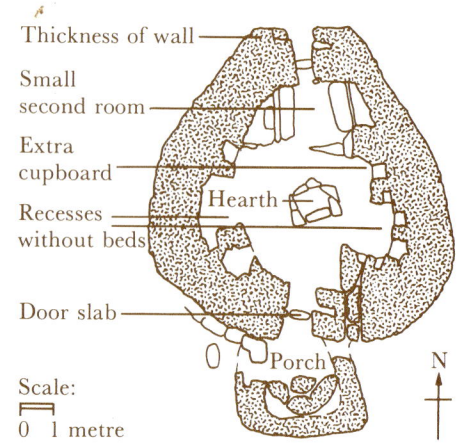

Thickness of wall
Small second room
Extra cupboard
Hearth
Recesses without beds
Door slab
Porch
Scale:
0   1 metre
N

A plan of hut 8. This shows the main parts of the hut. Check this plan with the clues.

Hut 8 at Skara Brae. Can you work out what it was used for?

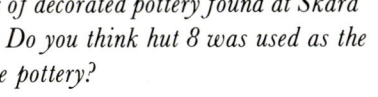

Pieces of decorated pottery found at Skara Brae. Do you think hut 8 was used as the village pottery?

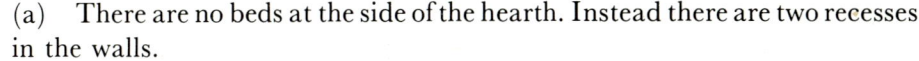

(a)   There are no beds at the side of the hearth. Instead there are two recesses in the walls.

(b)   There is an extra cupboard with two shelves on the right hand wall.

(c)   There are no stone boxes let into the floor for storing limpets in water.

(d)   No household objects were found in the hut.

(e)   There is no dresser opposite the doorway. Instead a gap in the wall opens into another small room, just over 2 metres square. The floor of this room is packed with stones, much cracked by heating. Many more of these stones were found outside, but not in other huts.

(f)   Large numbers of flint flakes and scrapers were found on the floor, as well as the flints used to shape other flint tools. These were not found in other huts.

(g)   At least part of the roof seems to have been made of stone.

(h)   A heap of yellow clay was found within the hut.

(i)   An unusually high number of stones in the hut were marked with patterns or designs.

What can these clues tell you about the use of hut 8? Archaeologists have had some ideas, but they disagree. One idea is that the villagers used the hut as the village kitchen. Another is that it was the village workshop. A third idea is that it was a potter's workshop.

Do you agree or disagree with any of these ideas, or do you have a different theory? Before deciding, you must test the ideas against the clues. What evidence is there for each idea?

In the last two chapters you have looked at the ways in which historians and other writers have reconstructed life in the past. You have also used clues for yourself when you worked on hut 8 at Skara Brae. In the next chapter you will have the chance to build up a picture of life at the Glastonbury lake village. You will use the information found at the site.

4: Glastonbury Lake Village

One day in 1892 Arthur Bulleid, a local man with a great interest in archaeology, was exploring marshland near Glastonbury in Somerset. Crossing a field, he realised that the ground he was walking over wasn't as flat as it looked from the road. The field wasn't ridged by ploughing. Instead it seemed to be full of very low, circular mounds. Checking the ground more carefully, Bulleid was helped by the work of very small but expert diggers — moles! Tunnelling through the soil, they had brought small pieces of bone and charcoal to the surface. Bulleid had found what he had been searching for!

Some lake or marsh villages had already been found in Europe. Bulleid had become very interested in these settlements and had been trying to find the same sort of village in England. He knew the kind of place to look in, and he set out to explore the marshes in the Glastonbury area. His interest uncovered one of the most important archaeological sites in Britain.

The site of the Glastonbury lake village. No wonder it was difficult to find!

Using information found at Glastonbury, we can build up this picture of lake village people sailing a canoe.

By the time excavations ended in 1907 knowledge about daily life in the Iron Age had greatly increased.

Before the full excavation began, Bulleid made one remarkable discovery. There were a number of modern drains in the area that often needed to be cleaned out. Bulleid asked the workmen if they had ever found anything very old. One man remembered a wooden beam that had jutted out into a drain. To keep the drain clear he had cut off the wood that stuck out. Although that had been eight years earlier he found the place again. When the 'beam' was dug out it was found to be a canoe, complete except for the part cut off by the workman. It was 5 metres long, more than half a metre wide, and had been cut whole from a tree trunk around 2000 years earlier.

A plan of the lake village. It shows the mounds and the palisade.

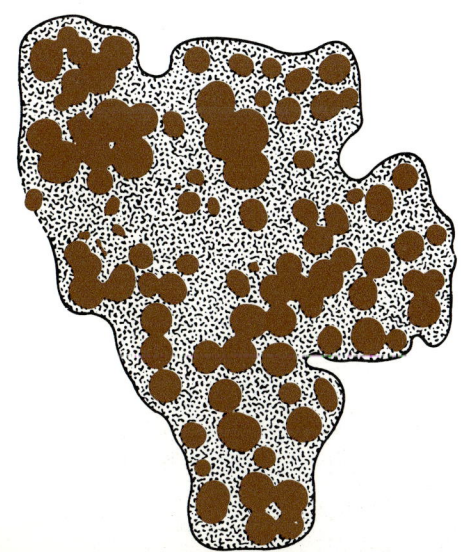

The archaeologists were not able to decide when people first lived at the Glastonbury site. The objects found there told them that it was inhabited about 2000 years ago, about the time of the birth of Christ. As more and more objects were found, the archaeologists realised that there were no Roman articles on the site. The Romans had invaded Britain in AD 43 and had taken over the Glastonbury area by about AD 50. Does this information tell you when people last lived in the Glastonbury village?

The site of the lake village is triangular. The village was not built in water but on a layer of peat next to a lake or marsh. Between the peat and the houses was a foundation of brushwood, logs and trees, stones, and rushes. A palisade or wooden wall stood around the village. This was made of timbers as long as 3½ metres. These timbers were held together by brushwood and hurdlework.

Before we look at the objects found at Glastonbury, think back to the finds from the other sites. What clues would you expect to find at a site like Glastonbury? What questions would these clues help you to answer? What questions do you think you won't be able to answer?

One of your first questions was probably, 'What kind of housing did these people have?' Do you expect to be able to answer this question? Remember, there were no clues about shelter at Star Carr, but plenty from the stone settlement at Skara Brae.

You have already seen the clue to the lay-out of the houses in the village. Look back at the plan on page 37. Did you wonder if the mounds marked houses? If you did, you were right! Each of the 89 mounds was the site of a house. However, only twenty or thirty houses were in use at any one time. People seem to have moved around the site as we might move from one street to another.

Here are the clues from the Glastonbury mounds. What do they tell you about the houses in the village?

(a)   The mounds were made of clay and ranged from 7½ centimetres to 2¾ metres in height. They varied from 4 to 12 metres in diameter. What was surprising was that the mounds weren't made of a solid layer of clay. They were made of layers of clay built on top of each other. Some layers were 60 centimetres thick. The chart on this page shows that some huts had a great many layers. Sometimes flat pieces of wood were found between the clay layers.

(b)   The shape of the mounds was marked by a series of holes in the ground. You can see here a plan of the holes from mound 45. In some holes broken-off wooden posts were discovered. Pieces of wattle were found between some of the holes. In the gap a piece of wood was found lying flat, and next to this was a number of pieces of stone, arranged to fit together.

(c)   In some mounds there was more than one set of holes. Whenever a mound was made of several layers of clay, there were several sets of holes.

(d)   The base of a post was found in the centre of a number of the mounds.

(e)   Some huts showed signs of having been burned down. Pieces of charred reed were mixed with the charcoal and ashes. Nowadays, reeds, rushes and heather grow near the site.

(f)   Round slabs of clay or stone were found near the centre of each mound. There was often a series of these slabs, built on top of each other. The largest number in any mound was thirteen. Sometimes the clay near these slabs had changed colour to a dark orange. In cracks in the slabs, pieces of baked clay, ash and charcoal were found.

This chart shows how many huts had more than one floor. Why do you think the huts had as many as ten floors?

Number of Floors	Number of Huts
1	23
2	22
3	21
4	13
5	3
7	4
8	1
9	1
10	1

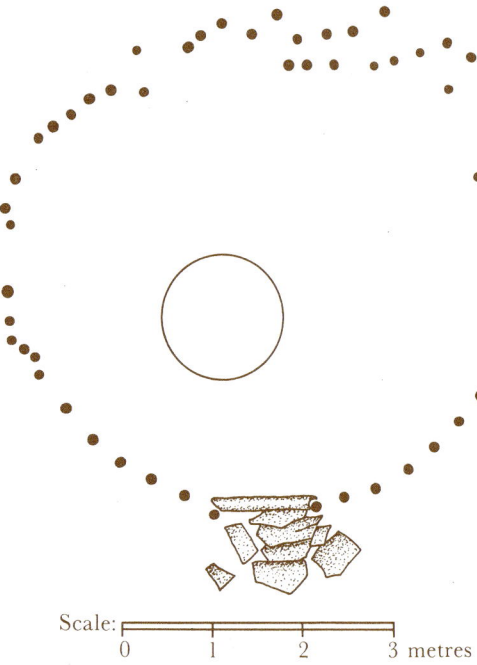

Scale:

0   1   2   3 metres

Plan of mound 45, described in clue (b)

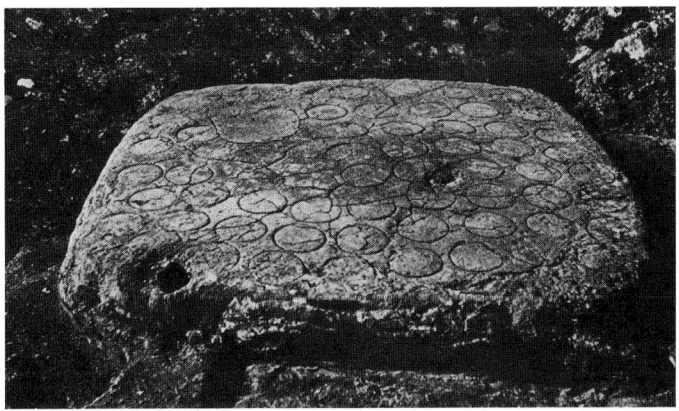

Wattle fencing of the type found at the lake village

One of the slabs of clay mentioned in clue (f)

What other information was found at Glastonbury?

On the next few pages you will find pictures and descriptions of many of the objects found at Glastonbury. What can you learn about the people of the village from this information?

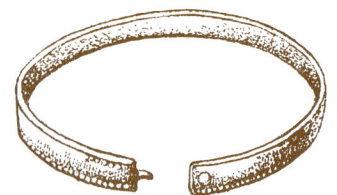

(4) Five bronze bracelets were uncovered, but only this one was complete. You can see the hook and eye used to close it.

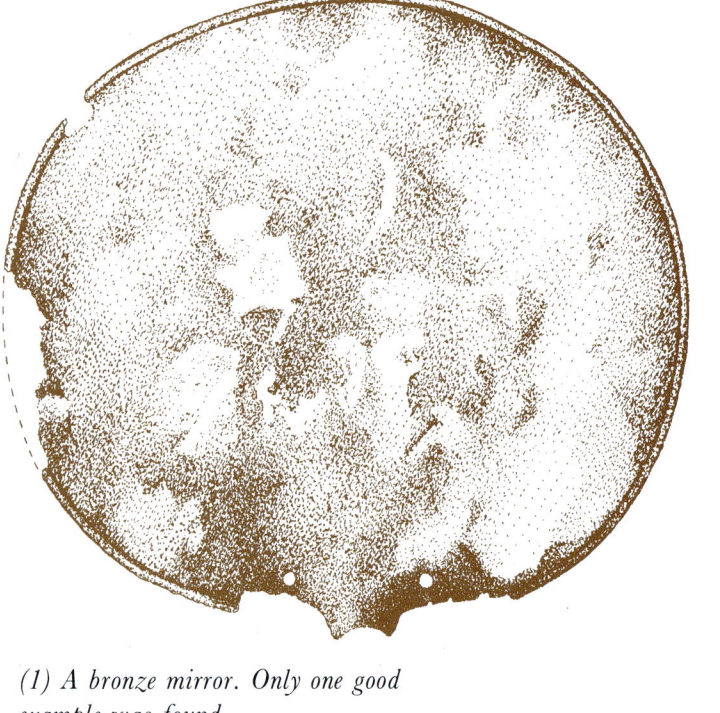

(1) A bronze mirror. Only one good example was found.

(5) Thirty-five bronze rings were discovered. The rings here show how they varied in size. The biggest ring has a diameter of 34 mm. The others have diameters of 21.5 mm, 16.7 mm and 12 mm.

(2) A small number of these bronze brooches were dug up. The decoration on them was very simple.

Scale:
0   5 cm

(3) Many needles made from bronze, bone and antler were discovered throughout the village.

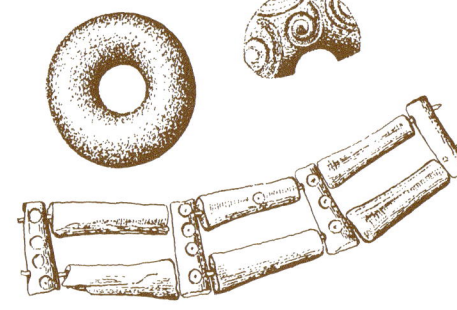

(6) There were five amber beads (coloured orange) and twenty-four glass beads. Most of the glass beads are plain blue but some, like the one shown here, are blue with white spiral shapes. A group of bone beads was also found. They formed the necklace shown here.

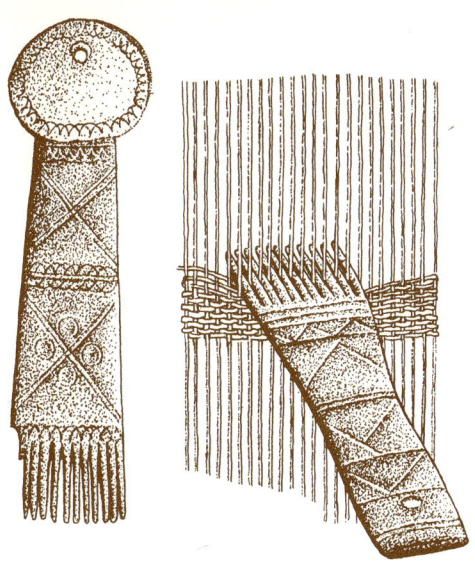

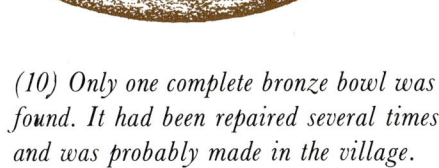

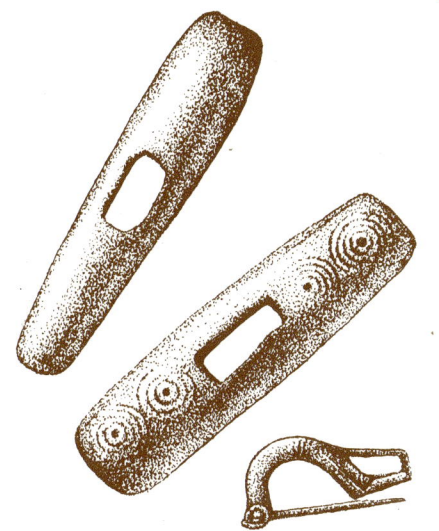

(7) Eighty-nine combs were found. Most of them were made from the antlers of red deer. Nine combs were found in one hut, seven combs in each of two other huts.

Above right you can see how the weaving comb was used to close up the weft threads (those running across). This made the cloth tighter and stronger.

(10) Only one complete bronze bowl was found. It had been repaired several times and was probably made in the village.

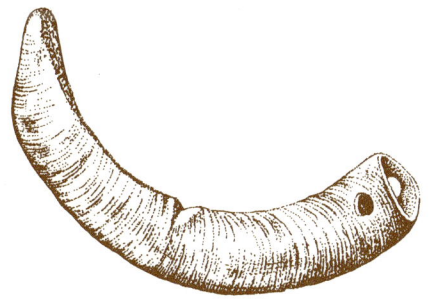

(8) A few tusks and teeth were found. Like this one, they had a single hole drilled in them but had no other decoration. The tusks came from boar.

(9) Several different kinds of fasteners were found, including over forty bronze fibulae. These acted as a kind of safety pin. There were also some toggles made from antlers.

(11) Two complete armlets and parts of eleven others were found. They were made of shale, a kind of stone. One of the complete armlets had had four cracks in it which had been repaired.

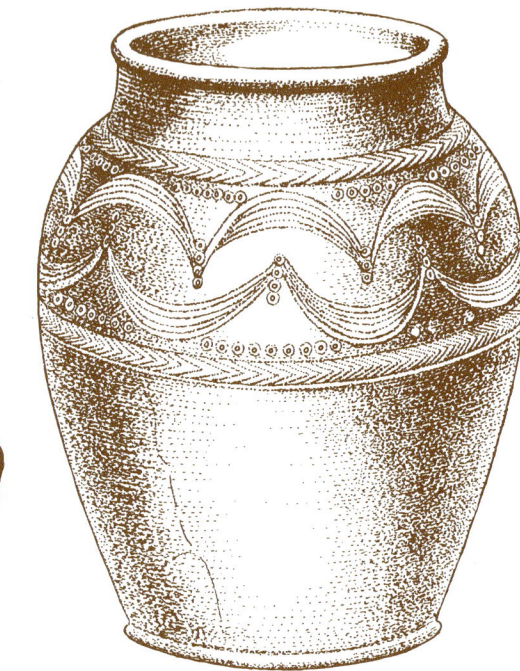

(14) Over 5000 pieces of pottery were found at Glastonbury. Half of them came from only ten mounds. Most were made by hand but some were made on a potter's wheel. These pictures show that the pots were both plain and decorated.

(15) Thirty-eight millstones like this one were found. These were used to grind corn to make flour. The corn was ground between a fixed lower stone and a top stone which was turned by hand.

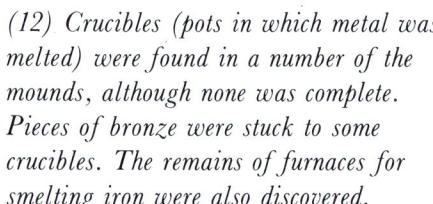

(12) Crucibles (pots in which metal was melted) were found in a number of the mounds, although none was complete. Pieces of bronze were stuck to some crucibles. The remains of furnaces for smelting iron were also discovered.

(13) This antler tool was used for carving the decorations on pottery.

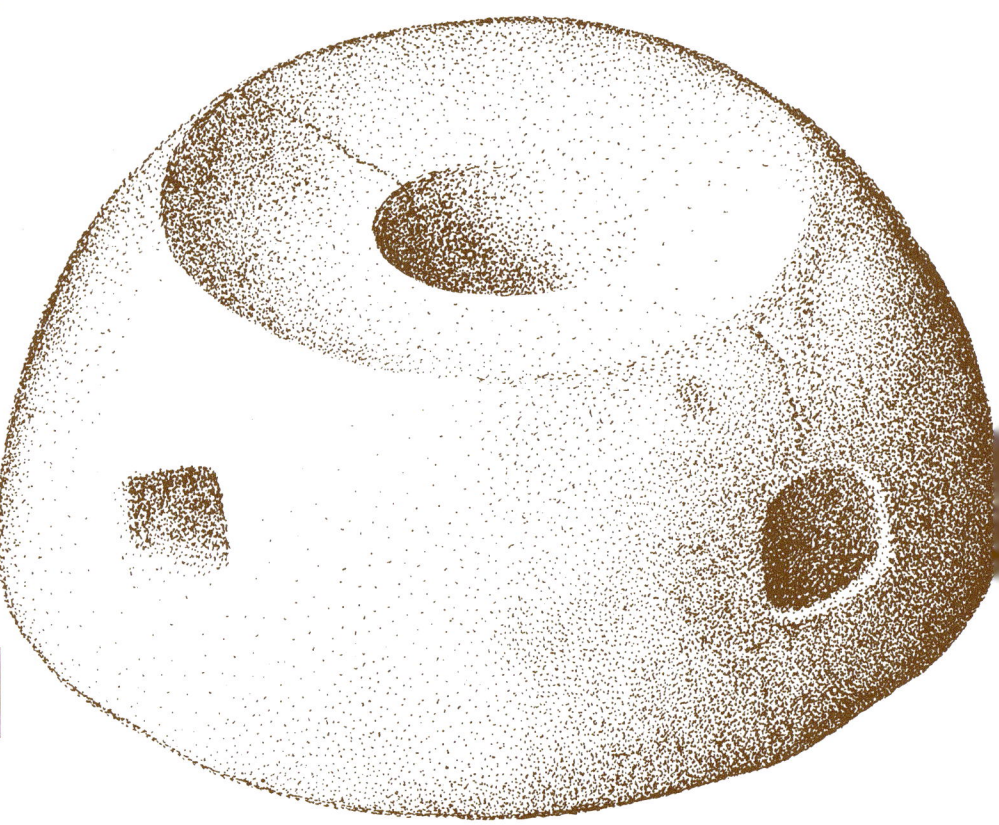

Scale:

0   10 cm

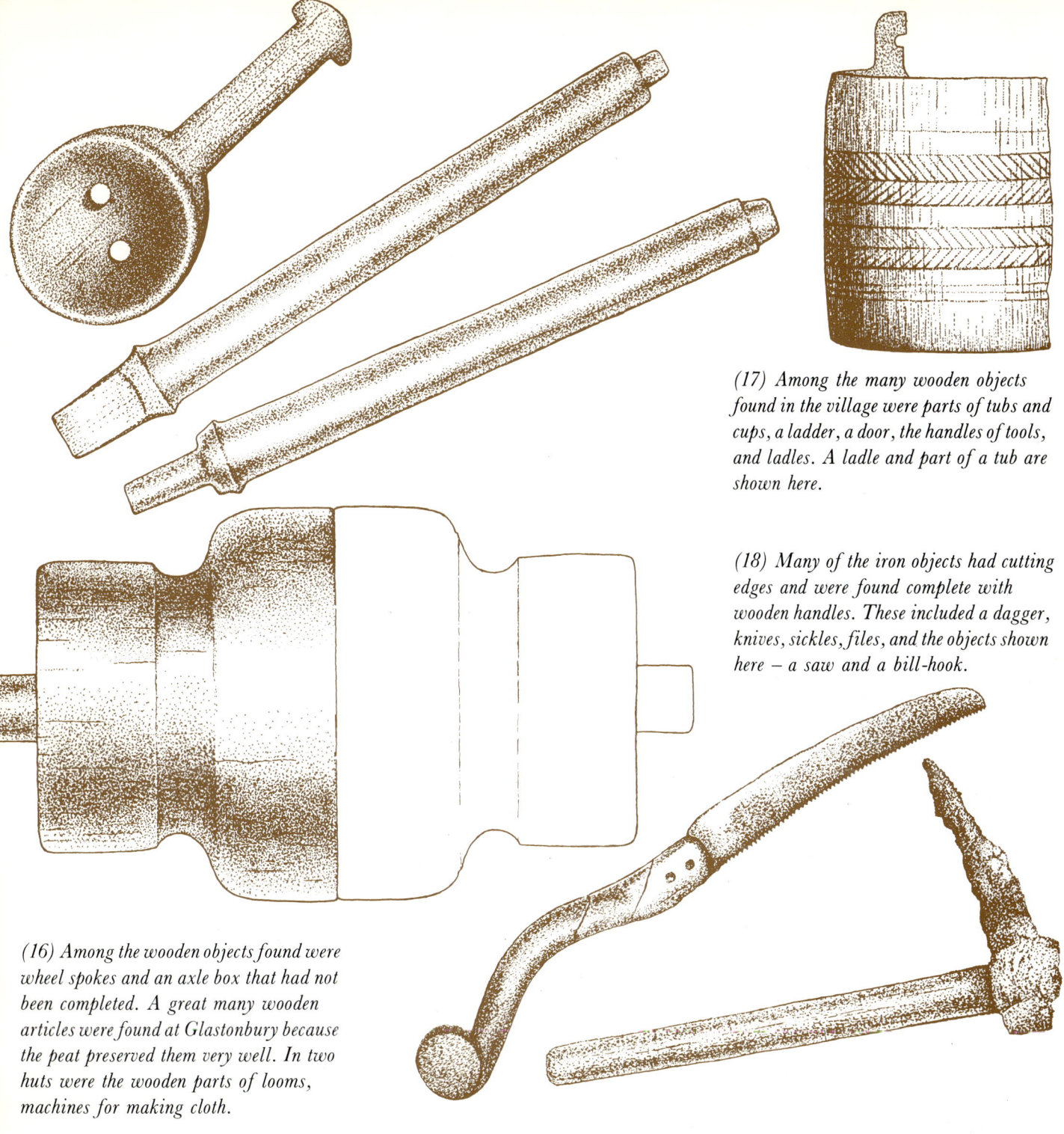

(17) Among the many wooden objects found in the village were parts of tubs and cups, a ladder, a door, the handles of tools, and ladles. A ladle and part of a tub are shown here.

(18) Many of the iron objects had cutting edges and were found complete with wooden handles. These included a dagger, knives, sickles, files, and the objects shown here – a saw and a bill-hook.

(16) Among the wooden objects found were wheel spokes and an axle box that had not been completed. A great many wooden articles were found at Glastonbury because the peat preserved them very well. In two huts were the wooden parts of looms, machines for making cloth.

5: Relics & Records

Glastonbury is a much larger site than Star Carr or Skara Brae. A far greater number and variety of objects were found there. These have helped you to decide what kinds of huts the Glastonbury villagers lived in. There are also plenty of examples of jewellery, pottery and woodwork, so we can see how skilful the people were. Although many items were left, there are still some things we don't know about the Glastonbury villagers. Why is this?

The main reason is that objects have survived only by accident. At Star Carr the hunters didn't leave things so that we would find them. Most remains are worn-out objects that the people did not need any longer, or they are things that people lost. At Skara Brae a sandstorm hid the buildings and stopped later people using the stones for their houses. These objects that are saved are known as *relics*.

Sometimes an accident can both help and hinder historians. The waterlogged ground of Glastonbury saved many wooden objects from rotting, but it destroyed other things like clothing. This leaves gaps in our knowledge.

Can we fill such gaps in our information? If an archaeologist has a question about Glastonbury that he can't answer he will look for another site like Glastonbury. Meare, another lake village near Glastonbury, is useful. It was lived in at the same time and its people had the same skills and customs. It might provide clues that were not found at Glastonbury.

Sometimes archaeologists find that there are people today who can help to answer their questions. This is because they still live in a way that is similar to that of people who lived long ago in Britain. You may remember that some questions about Star Carr (such as the use of the antler masks) were answered in this way.

A third way to find answers is very exciting. In chemistry we can repeat the great experiments made by scientists long ago. Archaeologists have also tried to experiment by building prehistoric settlements. There they test ideas about, for example, the Iron Age, the time when the Glastonbury lake village was inhabited.

One experiment is at Butser in Hampshire. There, archaeologists built huts to find out about building methods and how good the huts were as shelters. They grew Iron Age crops to see how much food they could get from them, and they used Iron Age tools to see how well these tools worked.

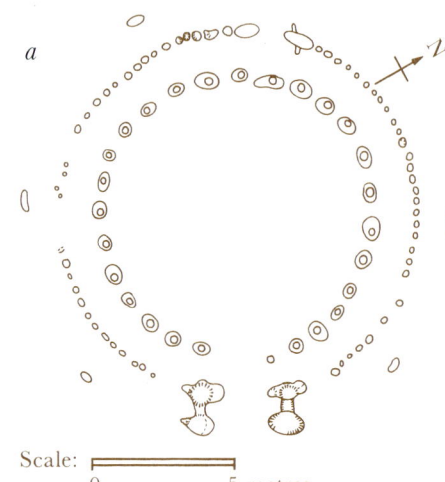

Scale:
0   5 metres

These pictures show stages of the building of a prehistoric round-house at Butser. Historians based their reconstruction on evidence from an excavation (a). They put the upright timbers exactly where they had found the post-holes (b); they constructed the rafters and beams (c); finally they added the roofing (d). This hut at Butser is the largest reconstruction of a prehistoric round-house ever built.

In all these ways archaeologists hope to fill gaps in our knowledge. However, there will always be questions that cannot be answered. We cannot expect to find out exactly what the people of Star Carr or Skara Brae looked like, what their names were, or how their language sounded. Did they have a village chief? What sorts of customs, beliefs or religion did they have? Did any of these people think it was sad or wrong to kill animals for food?

If you want to ask questions like these about any group of people in the twentieth century you can find the answers. Why can you do this for modern times but not for prehistoric Britain?

d

DOLLAR ACADEMY.

In this book we have looked at relics from thousands of years ago. Many more kinds of relics are left from the centuries since the Iron Age. We have Roman coins and Anglo-Saxon weapons, castles and manor-houses from the Middle Ages, machinery from nineteenth-century factories, clothes from the 1920s, and so on. All these are clues about the past but for these centuries we also have another kind of information.

The four sites studied in this book were built during the *prehistoric* period. What does 'prehistoric' mean? 'Pre' means 'before', so the whole word means 'before history' or, to make more sense, 'before history was written'. So these four places were built before anyone wrote a history of Britain. The first histories were written soon after the people left the Glastonbury village. The writers were Romans who had taken over the country.

Why did these Romans write about Britain? Perhaps they jotted things down to help their memories. Perhaps they wanted lots of people in Rome to hear about their success in Britain. Perhaps they were thinking of the future and wanted to leave the story of what the Roman people had done. Whatever the reason, Roman visitors recorded what they saw and described events in which they took part. We can call these deliberate writings *records*.

Records are not just written accounts. Nowadays we are used to recording events in many different ways — in paintings, in photographs, on film and on tape. Historians writing about Skara Brae do not have enough clues; historians of this century have a different problem — they often have too much information!

People of earlier times also found different ways of recording events. For example, the Egyptians used a kind of picture writing called hieroglyphics. Each picture stood for a sound or an object.

A famous example of Egyptian hieroglyphics. The name Tutankhamun was found on many objects in his tomb.

= *Amun* (the name of the god, *Amun*, comes first in the picture-writing)

= *Tut* (image)

= *Ankh* (life, or live)

Tut-ankh-amun (the living image of *Amun*)

= Ruler

= Southern

= On

Ruler of Southern On (Thebes)

46

An Incan official holding a quipu. A quipu had one main cord with many smaller, different-coloured strings attached to it. It was used to record events, pass messages, and keep accounts.

The Inca people of Peru recorded events on pieces of rope. Smaller cords hung from the main rope and knots were made in these strings. The knots could be 'read' only by Incan officials.

Records help historians a great deal. They can help to fill gaps in knowledge left by relics. Here's an example which can help us to learn a little more about the people of Glastonbury.

Julius Caesar led the first Roman armies to come to Britain. This is what he wrote about the Britons:

'All the Britons dye their bodies with woad, which produces a blue colour, and this gives them a more terrifying appearance in battle. They wear their hair long and shave the whole of their bodies except the head and the upper lip.'

We could never learn this kind of information from the relics at Glastonbury. Caesar's description helps us to imagine the people who lived at Glastonbury. Relics and records together help historians and archaeologists to gain as full a picture as possible. If only the builders of Stonehenge had known how to write!

'Well, this puts an end to prehistoric Britain!'

Relics to Records: the example of Star Carr